Passion
For Karate

Step – By – Step Guide to Starting your Karate Dojo

I0079311

Writer
James Giuliano

Creator: Giuliano, James - 1986 author
Title: Passion for Karate: Step - By - Step Guide to Starting your Karate Dojo
Subjects: Sports, Business

First paperback edition October 2020

Cover design by Booklerk
Illustrations by Kateryna Derevianko

ISBN 978-0-646-82628-8 (paperback)

www.mekakarate.com.au
Disclaimer

MEKA

KARATE

Contents

About the author

Focus, determination and persistence provide the foundation of the ethos of James Giuliano's life. An early introduction to these attributes is key to seeing the skills learnt through his Karate career influence his achievements and everyday life. Starting at age 6, in a local Karate dojo with his brothers, 'just for fun', little did James know the shape his life would take through and from the sport of Karate.

His decision to pursue Karate led James to a 28-year career that has seen him become a world-class athlete, train and compete internationally with many revered trainers and medal in countless tournaments and championships. James featured on the competitive circuits, winning the Italian and U.S Open Championships in 2014 and claiming his 10th Australian Championship title in 2016.

As life progressed and his passion for Karate continued to flourish into a serious career path, James applied the skills learnt through his sport into real life. From his determination at the age of 15 to have an impact on the Karate competition scene, to his passion to make a difference and inspire others: James is now the proud founder of a Melbourne based Karate school, this passion-turned-career now sees him imparting his knowledge and skills gained throughout his life with more than 300 students.

Through this journey of establishing his Karate school and developing age-appropriate programs, James' teaching philosophy and beliefs have evolved into one that centres on connection and meaningful interaction with his students. James focuses on developing confidence, self-belief and resilience through Karate and he has combined this with a systematic business approach to his teachings - the key to success, always being prepared for what lies ahead.

James has a depth of knowledge, experience and insights to share with the world through this book, and if that is not enough of a reason to read it following one person's journey to success through sheer determination is.

The Opportunity

Hi, I'm James Giuliano, co-founder of Liberte Karate and founder of Meka Karate. This is the story of my journey in opening up a karate school with a difference. I've spent a large part of my life in martial arts, and in travelling the world, competing and training at the highest of levels, while building a strongly cultured karate school in Australia.

This book is designed to help guide karate practitioners to becoming the best they can be. I provide you with a vision you may never have thought possible, in running a successful and profitable karate school, without it taking over your life. Here, I cover all of the do's and do-nots of teaching, and I provide support for your journey to teach at the highest of levels. I simplify my teaching to help you understand and to adapt in the quickest possible manner. In this chapter, I will introduce myself to those who don't know me, and I will tell the story of my journey in karate.

Before we get started, it's important to understand that in karate we must learn from one another and to respect each other along the way. With that said, let's start at the beginning...

For over 15 years, I pursued my dream to become one of the world's top competitors, and I represented Australia on the international stage to 2016. I had my successes and I wound up with something that I never anticipated: something that would impact me for the rest of my life—a sport that would provide me with endless passion and opportunity.

Throughout all those competing years, I learned the enjoyment of helping other athletes achieve their best, and the satisfaction of my having inspired young students to reach for the stars.

Over this one-and-a-half decade journey, I committed everything I had to achieving my personal goals, and I learned about the ups and downs of life. I started to develop a philosophy of continuous development—of setting small goals to attain a big vision.

Over this time, I won eleven Australian titles, ranking in the top eight at two world championships, and I won many international competitions along the way.

At the age of 25, I started to think about my future and what I would do once I retired from competition. I began to observe as many karate instructors as I could, and what I saw certainly didn't inspire me, as many lacked passion and were financially insecure. It didn't seem as though karate was a good business to be in, so I didn't give it much thought.

By chance, I caught up with a friend for coffee and we started playing with the question of *What if?* What if we opened a karate school? What would it look like? We were not just interested in *how* it would look, but more importantly, at the culture of the school. What would it be like for everyone? By everyone, we meant the entire karate school community, and there are a lot of people involved. A karate school should not just be about the students, but also the parents, the students' friends, and definitely the instructors themselves. We wondered how we could run it as a business and still maintain integrity. Was there potential for karate as a business? We decided the answer was a definite Yes!

Then, I had to define what success really meant to me.

I developed the Six Levels of Dojo Success:

- One: Like any business, it had to make a profit.

- Two: There would be no compromising of personal philosophies.

- Three: There must be a strong work/life balance.

- Four: Customer service would require our focus on quality over quantity.

- Five: The development of a community spirit was paramount.

- Six: Everyone involved must have fun, and benefit from the sport of karate.

Now, you can move those six levels around and place them in any order you like, it doesn't matter. They are all essential and all support each other.

This business concept was for a lifestyle business. The general idea was to run a karate school supported by all the necessary processes to ensure passion for it wouldn't diminish over time.

I knew that a method of teaching karate that would excite the new generation of children was paramount, and I knew I wanted to build something special that would change children's lives.

With this in mind, I moved forward on a course that nobody believed I could achieve in such a short period of time.

Through my travels, I had been exposed to different teaching methods and it was in Italy that I was really impressed.

In 2010, I had just competed and won Bronze in the prestigious Italian Open. At the time, placing at this particular competition was a highlight of my career. But when I reflected on my time there, I realised that what I had gained most was not winning, but what I had learned.

While training, I noticed the Italian Karate Federation had developed an amazing training program that focused on children's motor skill development—a new and fresh approach to teaching. This inspired me for years to come.

I knew I had to bring this methodology back to Australia, where everyone was still training traditionally. This could become the start of a product difference to our competitors, and something I could mould into a program suitable for Australian children.

The goal that I was inspired to pursue was to develop co-ordination skills first, so that when we teach a student a karate technique, they find it easy to learn, and in turn it becomes more enjoyable. If a child finds something too difficult to grasp, the challenge becomes too great and they quit. The simple fact is, that if students find karate techniques easy to learn, the chances that they will enjoy the sport are significantly higher.

I have always said that if a student enjoys what they do, they will train for longer periods of time and achieve big goals, so that became our aim: to keep students developing their skills.

We more generally see a lot of traditional programs that were created years ago in Japan, and that are based on the Japanese culture.

The question is: Who are we targeting? Japanese adults? Japanese children? or Australian children? There is a big difference between these demographics.

The Japanese culture differs from our Australian culture. Australians enjoy training in a more relaxed environment. Our kids are not likely to train for three hours a day every day, and that is important to understand.

I wanted to develop a program that children enjoyed, and my program must still retain a core focus on traditional karate values. I adapted an old school syllabus into an engaging modern-day program that was specifically developed for children.

I was aware that it's not *what* you teach, but *how* you teach that becomes the key factor. This philosophy became a core difference between us and our competitors and the karate industry.

From those realisations, I developed a business plan, along with a program for students, and I offered two nights of training.

Starting from scratch, the plan was a first on many levels, and it was the first time we would be teaching children from a beginner's level. I thought I knew it all, considering how long I'd been training. I thought it would be easy.

I remember teaching a five-year-old boy, Jack, who was a white belt and I assumed this would be so simple. I started to teach Jack basic kata #1. I performed the moves and assumed that he would simply copy me and perform the kata. To no avail though, as Jack didn't know his left from his right, let alone how to do a basic stance.

I had a long way to go! I made mistake after mistake over the following five years, but I continued to improve the program and processes and I never stopped moving forward.

I could see where students struggled with the current syllabus and I evaluated why this was the case, then made changes, whether that was to the syllabus program or to teaching practices. This ensured that future students would not have the same problems. This *continuous development* was undertaken until finally a syllabus and program was developed that harnessed students' strengths instead of presenting hurdles too large to overcome.

I had a vision, and I would do anything necessary to reach it.

Over the next five years I developed better and better teaching practices, and ours became one of the strongest karate schools in our community.

Another factor that was very important to our success, was in ensuring the instructors kept their passion alive on a long-term basis and, just like the students, avoided burnout. To be successful, this element had to be our priority, because without passionate instructors, you don't have a viable school.

How do we keep instructors passionate? The answer is straightforward: by investing and valuing them as an integral part of the business. That means not taking advantage of them, but making sure that we're always doing what's best for our instructors and the school. The guiding principle was to never take anyone for granted and to value the people who helped develop our school. It's an integral fact that all the best energy should be used for all the best results.

Most large dojos have been around for 20 years and have taken a long-term approach to growth. We were able to hit our goals of near maximum capacity of 250+ students in five years, as well as developing a strong culture within our karate school: something I'm very proud of.

Why did I choose to open a karate school?

I believe doing something you are passionate about is so important, and my passion is karate and in helping inspire people to achieve their goals. These objectives led me to my next chapter in life.

Teaching children is incredible, and provides great satisfaction. You can be yourself, and be playful, with no façade to being someone you're not. You have the chance to make an impact on someone's life and to help shape the person they will become. It's an amazing feeling when you know you have a proven program that impacts your students' lives, in and outside of karate.

My aim was to run a karate school that had a positive impact on the community, as well as being financially viable, while providing a stress-free and family-friendly lifestyle of passion and commitment, and... *bingo*!

Teaching karate in my own school has given me the flexible lifestyle I was looking for, where I could have another job on the side, if that's what I wanted. It's all about creating flexibility to do the things you love.

The vision was that as an instructor, each week I would turn up to class with a plan to follow and everything ready to go, and that I could enjoy the event. At night's end, I would pack up, go home and relax, until the next night of training. In between, all the running of the business had been taken care of. I was free to do what I liked from day to day: keeping fit, reading books and simply enjoying life. While I'm no longer competing, this would allow me to stay connected with something I have participated in all my life.

Looking back at my teen years and early twenties, I grew up in a family that ran small businesses. That was where I learned the importance of customer service, the need for a strong product, and having processes in place that ran the business smoothly.

This knowledge led me to my vision of a karate school that would run like a business, rather than one that relied on making decisions on the go. This would be a part of my point of difference to my competitors, and something I would base success upon.

Planning allows everyone involved to stay fresh and passionate. It is hard to maintain enthusiasm for something when you are being drained by business needs

that you didn't at first perceive. I have seen good karate teachers become exhausted, not because they trained too long, but because they lacked processes to support them. They, like many that go into different small businesses, lacked the knowledge to actually run a small business.

The program created would need to set the layout for each and every night of teaching and would link to a structured calendar for the year, and thus it would help create a positive flow in the teaching of our students.

There are times for students to work hard, times for them to have fun, and times to develop their performance. This can't be done randomly. An efficient program needs a great deal of thought and understanding of what works best, and this must be based on experience.

My aim is to keep it simple for instructors so that they simply turn up and teach. It's similar to an elite athlete's program, with its ebbs and flows to ensure they achieve the best they can, but to be effective, a program must be followed.

After six years, my karate school was running effortlessly and then with MEKA KARATE, it was time to pass on my knowledge. It was time to create a guide for other Instructors to open their own karate schools, with the backing of a tried and true system and program that's been developed over years.

Any karate style can be adapted to this program and everyone will have their own personality and way of teaching that will make them different to other schools around them. The support system is there to help you through the journey.

The main aims of MEKA KARATE are to create an opportunity for you to do something you are passionate about, to be financially rewarded, and to create flexibility so that you have spare time, and to keep fit, stay healthy and follow other life goals that you wish to achieve.

The commitment needed has been developed for you to take up as a part-time commitment.

It could be difficult to develop a karate school when you have a full-time job. You would be required to learn marketing strategies, to develop class structures, and to deal with all that goes with running a business, making it impossible to manage whilst simultaneously working full time.

Meka Karate offers a new system, something for all karaticas, something unique. It's about sharing knowledge and inspiring others, so that we can create something special and impact children across the country. It's about mentoring: mentoring instructors and then instructors becoming mentors to their students... and so the cycle continues.

This is something I believe will be revolutionary in karate. It's time for the those passionate about the sport to open up and connect with each other.

With a proven record for success, it's now time to share my knowledge.

In this chapter, I hope I've given you something to think about—something you may have never thought was even a possibility—and to help you reflect on your personal journey in karate and where it may lead into the future.

Karate doesn't have to end after reaching a black belt, it doesn't have to end after competing.

The Opportunity

Karate is more than a sport, it's a lifestyle, and it's there to help us become better people, providing us with an opportunity to make change in this world.

What is the spirit of karate?

The spirit of karate resides in why you do karate *or* why you love karate. This realisation will be important when there are times of struggle. At such times, it may help to remember why you love karate and why you want to teach others. You may discover that this will be the same reason that kept you training at karate for all those years.

My sense of karate spirit speaks to my core principles in karate, which are: the development of someone's focus, respect and preparation. These principles lead to helping someone create a sense of self-belief.

If I had to sum up why I love karate in four words, they would be: Learning, Developing, Sharing and Inspiring . All four freely given, with no ego and with friendship.

The spirit of karate will be found in that moment that you help your student and they wear the *Wow, I can do this* look! Your rewards will come in helping people achieve their goals when they thought it was all too difficult. The spirit of karate is that proud feeling when you have impacted someone in a positive way.

The spirit of karate is all the good things in karate that in turn create passion.

The spirit of karate is in teaching how to create strong discipline to achieve set goals, while overcoming distractions by setting a strong focus. These objectives also become life skills and will help students outside of the karate program and we, in turn, become mentors as well as teachers, guiding them to become good people.

Conclusion

Often, people don't think about why they do something or perform a particular behaviour. I hope this chapter has opened your mind and you have learned something about yourself here. I'm sure some points will have resonated with your ideals. The spirit of karate for you is an important factor to consider before opening a karate school. The end goal is for happiness. If you follow this pathway rather than following the money, you will be sure to have a successful school that you will be proud to own, and you will deserve all the rewards that come with it.

What makes a great karate instructor?

It is important to understand where you need to develop your skills to become a great instructor. It took me years of teaching before I understood what made me into that person, so I will share the elements with you, some of which may seem new. Below are some concepts to get your mind ticking over, to create a thought process about who you are as a person, and why you do what you do.

Firstly, a passion for karate must be your primary motivator. If you embark upon instructing for the dollars alone, then you will never tick the boxes you need to tick in order to achieve a great outcome for yourself and for others. I found that my passion led me to teach more, and the more I taught, the more I relaxed, which led me to enjoy teaching karate more.

Secondly, is the passion to teach children. You need to enjoy helping others and in particular, in helping children become great karaticas and perhaps even more importantly, in mentoring them to become the people they will become as they grow up. For me, teaching children is great—they don't judge you, and you can feel completely relaxed when teaching them. If you set strong guidelines, you can be their friend while also gaining their respect, which will ultimately ensure they heed your teachings.

Thirdly, is having the passion to be a mentor. Helping somebody move forward in their life will provide you with a strong sense of achievement. I have been mentored myself, and I have gained so much from it over the years that it became something I wanted to do for others. The best part about being a mentor is that you can help someone through their journey, helping to navigate them through their ups and downs. For students, this can be as simple as ensuring you maintain communication with students on how they are travelling in karate. One day you will look back at a student and feel confident that you had an impact on who they became as an adult. You will have done this through the core principles of karate.

We also need the commitment to encourage change, which is another reason why you make the choice to mentor others. I didn't realise when I first started my karate school that changing children's lives would have an impact on them and on me. When the evidence of it happened the first time, it took me by surprise, and then became the most important driving force for me as a teacher.

I remember a particular boy, Tommy, and the day he started training at my school. When he joined our class, his coordination was something that he really needed to work on. Simply jumping on two feet (kumite bounce) without losing balance was even a challenge for Tommy. I was determined that this student was going to make it to the end of the term without quitting, so considering everyone else was developing at a much faster rate, I spoke with him about being patient, about setting small goals, and about focusing on his journey, and not the journey of others. We set our goals for the term and he was on his way. He stayed focused and stuck to his plan. He listened to instructions, and over time without even knowing, something clicked, and he started to get better and better as the term went along. Eventually, I called him out of class for a chat. I asked him to perform his kumite bounce, which was something he had struggled with for so long. There he was, achieving the task without realising that he was doing his kumite bounce perfectly.

At that point, I wanted Tommy to reflect on how far he had travelled, at where he had first started, and to see what he had achieved. It may have seemed like a small improvement, but I knew it would be symbolic for his life. I explained to him that in his life he may find things difficult, but now he understood the method to succeed: to stay focused, to set small goals, and not to compare himself with others. I convinced him that if he did this, he could achieve anything. That experience with Tommy changed the way I saw teaching. The look in his eyes conveyed that he suddenly knew he was able to do something in his life that he may not have thought was possible. Now, imagine that impact with a whole school of children, then you will understand.

An obvious element to becoming a great instructor is that you need to be fun and exciting, which will ensure you connect with the children. By opening up and being yourself, you will gain their trust and show that you're there for them. You're like a friend, and at the same time you have a strict code of behavior that you require from the students. For example, I will be playing a game and having fun, and then it's time to move onto some technical training. Being able to switch from fun to serious is important, so that the students can listen to your instructions with intent—it's all about building trusted relationships.

The fourth stage of becoming a great instructor is in learning how to motivate a student to make them feel inspired. It's not something you need to be a natural at, but understanding the importance of this factor is crucial. The philosophy behind it is that if you're asking a child to come in and work hard for you, the least you can do is provide positive feedback when they progress. This knowledge, that they are progressing and moving forward, will translate to a positive association with their karate practice.

I have a student named Kylie in my class. Kylie isn't a natural, but she makes up for it with her commitment and passion to become better. She had been having some trouble developing the new section of her kata. (There are sections of kata that students need to learn as a component of their next belt requirements, and sometime these can be quite challenging.) I had shown her how to do it, step-by-step, and then she needed to practice with repetition so that she would eventually perform this section correctly. She struggled at first, so I kept motivating her by telling her not to give up, and I kept guiding her through this process. Her parents confirmed to me that she had been practicing at home, which was great to hear. She then came to me in class and asked me to check out her performance. She *smashed* it, with perfect technique and confidence. I took her aside to create a positive buzz in that moment.

I needed to make Kylie feel that every time she performed that particular section, she would remember that positive reinforcement in her mind, that feeling that she believes in herself and that she's a great student. I called Kylie out and told her that the section she performed was amazing. I said, 'You're on fire!' and I give her a high five. I added, 'You know you put in the hard work and now you're at the next level'. The excitement in her eyes—just like Tommy's—said it all: that she was loving training with me. You need to do this every time someone makes a big step forward, because that's what keeps them motivated. This can be done in all aspects of training. It's important they feel great when they achieve a goal, and that's your job.

Just knowing this will help you become a better instructor, and it comes with experience, so the more you do it, the better you will become. Believing in what you're doing is crucial. Understanding why you do what you do is vital.

The elements of Passion

ELEMENT #1 → Passion for Karate

+

ELEMENT #2 → Passion to teach

+

ELEMENT #3 → Passion to Inspire and Mentor

Class structure and layouts: preparation is key

Layout and structure of the class are extremely important. It's not just about having a group of children in a class and filling up the numbers, then teaching whatever might be on your mind that day. Over the long term, without a set program for students to follow, that attitude would find you not retaining your students. As well, this style of teaching would be exhausting for an instructor who would always be needing to think up what to do next. That is a recipe for burnout.

Building up the numbers of students in a school isn't difficult. Retaining those students is the challenge, requiring the service on offer to be 100%. Excellent service will translate to students and parents who will become long term fans, which further translates to kids and parents loving what you do and how you do it. This leads to the best form of promotion and growth: word of mouth.

You would be surprised at what children are seeking in a karate class. All too often, karate instructors believe it's the amount of knowledge an instructor has that's most important. Although that is a part of a good school, it isn't what develops enthusiastic fans. More importantly, it's about how you connect with students through your method of teaching and communication. To achieve this, you will need a strong plan, excellent preparation, and sound structure in place at the outset, for you to follow over the course of a term.

One important element is a flowing class structure. Let us consider how important it might be to having age specific classes. When we first opened our school we didn't have a lot of students, so we invited everyone and anyone to join in the same class, so that we could avoid paying more rent for our hired venue. We tried to fit as many students as we could in one group, and soon found that having a twelve-year-old with a five-year-old simply didn't work. We then changed our class structure, to make smaller, age-specific classes, so that when a student joined, they felt comfortable training with students of the same age. This quickly became a discussion point for new students looking to join. At that time, providing age-specific classes was a point of difference with our competitors.

The way you communicate with a five-year-old is different to the way you communicate with a ten-year-old and therefore, placing them together creates conflict in the method of communication to all the students. We need to be able to connect with our students, as they all have individual needs and requirements. Having students train with others of similar age helps nurture the development of social skills, as the children are not then intimidated by older peers. Building social skills is a part of the karate journey.

To simplify it, think about the way you talk with your grandmother or grandfather compared with how you speak with a teenager. We adjust our communication style in our daily lives, so why wouldn't we do it in karate also.

The age groups that we have found works best in karate classes are noted here. While some do overlap to create flexibility, each can change and overlap depending on skill level and the maturity of a class.

- Five and six years
- Six to eight years
- Eight to ten years
- Ten to twelve years
- Eleven to thirteen years
- Fourteen years and over

Class duration for students is important. Our goal is to have a class with high impact, high intensity and students ending each class wanting more. Often our students say, 'Are we finished already?' and that is usually followed up with me saying, 'Time flies when you're having fun!'

The truth is that we could teach more in a longer class, but we are looking at the long game here: we want our students eager to come back to every class with positive energy, rather than thinking, 'How long to go until we're finished?' If we push them too much, they will burn out, and it won't matter how much they know, it's irrelevant if they quit. Also, you will find that if the students are exhausted, the instructor becomes exhausted as well. A class needs to be enjoyable for all involved.

Forty-minute classes are ideal as this allows the program to provide high intensity and a fun environment for our students. As they become older—at the age of fifteen—this can be extended to an hour, depending on the types of students in the class.

Another element to a positive class structure is parents staying out of the room but still watching. We find that initially when a student starts training, the parents always stay and watch. Eventually, once the students have been there for a long time, you find parents watch less and less, although of course you still have the keen parents who always like to watch. I have found that parents watching class is a positive thing, but it is important we try to have a separate audience area to avoid parents distracting the students while they are training, for example, with chatter or other noise such as siblings running around.

Rules and Boundaries

For your structure and class layout to be executed perfectly, you need to set rules and boundaries for the students. Our goal in class is to understand each individual's needs and help develop students in a group environment. As an example, if a student is disruptive and not listening to your instructions, you must set boundaries and rules. If they don't follow these rules, then you will need to implement consequences. At the same time, you must explain to the child or children why they are receiving consequences and how they can move forward from that point. The worst thing you can do is to not implement rules, which could see you exhausted from chasing some students around the class and other students not receiving any of your attention. At the start, students need to learn your expectations, and they need to see that you are serious about the dojo rules.

If someone breaks the rules multiple times, they should get warnings, and then may sit out for some time during the class. You would discuss with them the importance of following the rules and why it is important, and if their behaviour continues, then so will the consequences. You will then find that they either adapt to your class rules and structure or they will quit. Your commitment to rules will ensure flexibility in your classes and you will be able to enjoy your teaching a lot more. Also, once the rules are implemented with all of your students, you will find when a new student joins, they will see other students' behaviour and follow suit. It becomes easier the longer your classes are running.

Why prior planning of a class layout is important and how it led us to success.

Our goal is for students to have a great time, and equally importantly, the instructor's enjoyment is just as crucial. We want to reach the end of the year with just as much motivation and energy as when we started. We have a strong understanding of the potential for instructor burnout so this is why we plan ahead.

If you remove all the instructor's concerns about running a class, including: what needs to be done? who next to be taught what? and how will I teach it? you will create stress-free teaching and develop a good flow in classes. If it's planned, you're able to look at the structure, look at the flow, and implement a plan of action that will provide the best quality service possible to our customers.

MAKING IT EASY
WITH CLASS LAYOUTS

The alternative would be like playing in a football game with no game plan and everyone just playing what and how they feel is best. You can see how difficult it would be to achieve the goal to win. Karate classes are no different—well for us anyway. Having a plan allows us to achieve our objective: to provide the best karate classes possible.

Class structure and layouts: preparation is key

Class layouts are developed at the start of each term. Classes are evaluated, and a plan is set in place based on a student's development. There are four terms in a year, which allows us to evaluate and adapt our plan on four occasions. This sets up great flow throughout the whole term and is a key principle to our success in implementing continuous improvement across all facets of the business.

By setting up these layouts, we allow the instructor to relax and focus on their daily lives without needing to worry about what's happening next week and the week after that. Over time, that sort of concern builds up and creates stress—something we want to avoid. This is a huge point of difference to other karate schools and we are yet to find one that implements this amount of detail in their program.

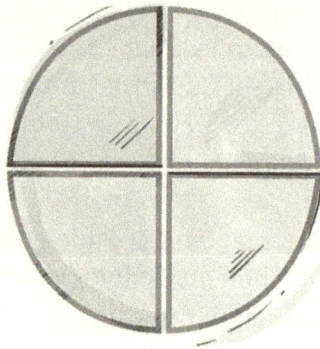

Core principles to success

When I reflect upon the journey from first opening my karate school and the eight years that followed, I have asked myself: Where did our success come from? Was it developed over time or was it there from the start? I came to see that everything I did to build the business was led by four core principles, and I found that these principles were embedded into all sectors of our business. Below, I reflect upon these principles and how we implemented them into our teachings for our students. These principles are all about *why* I love to teach karate, and I believe now it was this that led to our success as a business, even if we didn't know it at the time. The first three principles are aimed at students, and the fourth is aimed at the teacher.

Principle #1 – Establishing a Strong Focus

In everything I do, I've always had a concentrated focus when working towards a goal. I learned this while training for five world championships and then understood that this focus can be used in a variety of ways.

In training students, we wanted to teach them how to create a very strong focus in pursuit of a specific goal, such as achieving their black belt. Once a student starts to achieve their goals, we can link it to other aspects of their lives, including school and work, etc. The plan is to teach skills that have lasting effects and help a child develop into a strong, confident and independent person.

We have two stages of focus: Stage One is a focus that sets strong concentration. This allows a student to block out distractions and stay focused. We call this the *ready position*, which allows the student to stay in the moment and perform a selected task. This might be performing kata or even kumite, and the better focus they have, the more confidence they gain, which leads to the development of better long-term confidence and self-belief.

Stage Two is what I call *moving focus*. Picture a student in a ready position stance with strong concentration, the next step is to enter moving phase focus. The student can now isolate a thought, for example: I want to push off from my left foot and step fast into my stance and at the same time, not be distracted, while I hold strong concentration. This leads into moving focus, having more than one thought at a time and executing it. This is all about how to perform to the best of your ability under pressure... something I learned over many years of performing.

If you can teach this to children, they will become good at karate. They will be able to perform strongly and build a powerful sense of self-belief.

Once again, this is a skill that will filter into children's lives as they grow up. They will have goals and they'll come across hurdles, but if they have developed a strong sense of concentration and focus, they will avoid distractions and always find a way to progress. This is the message we pass onto all students and parents.

Principle #2 – Understanding the key element of Preparation

The next principle is preparation. We want to teach our children that, no matter how difficult something is, if they are well prepared, then they have a higher potential to succeed in achieving a specific goal.

For example, I had a student named Melissa, who was very shy when performing in front of others, and it was time for her to enter the local competition. We ran this competition for the sole purpose of building confidence in our students. Melissa's mum called up to say Melissa didn't want to enter as she had a fear of performing and failing in front of others. In the next class, I spoke with Melissa and discussed how to perform in front of others, and with confidence. I discussed with her that she was good enough to compete, but we simply had to work on our preparation. I explained to her over the next two weeks that she was to practice at home in preparation for the competition. I told her then and there to visualise herself walking out and performing her kata at the competition. Once she did this, I ask her to then perform the kata at home, again pretending she was at the competition. With repetition, this would give her confidence while creating some perceived pressure. I told her to repeat this three times a week at home. This would create strong preparation for the competition and help develop her confidence.

Melissa continued to follow our plan of attack, and on competition day she performed marvellously, winning Gold in her division. We were excited by what she had achieved, so I had a chat with her about where she had come from and what had helped her perform confidently. It was a simple message that she understood: if you prepare for something, it will give you the self-belief that you can achieve something you thought was not possible.

Now the goal was to remember this situation for the next time she became nervous or when a peer was in the same position, and she could explain to them how to move forward positively through having strong preparation.

I often use this strategy for my students before a grading, so that everyone is well prepared to perform at their best on the day. We perform a mock grading whereby I put them under pressure and get them to rise to the occasion, to perform their best and give it 110%.

This is something I learned over a decade while competing at many world championships, and something that children can easily develop with the correct messaging from us. This core principle impacts our students in and out of the karate school. It may be applied when studying for an exam at school or when trying to achieve a large goal that they might have arise in their lives. Preparation for anything is key to becoming successful in achieving the desired goal.

Principle #3 – Establishing a strong sense of Respect

Respect has always been a traditional aspect of karate, and I believe over the years we have seen a revolution in the meaning of respect.

Through karate, I have learned the value of respecting others. Although in karate it can sometimes be seen as the image of a pyramid, in that you must respect anyone higher than you: this may be a higher Dan grade, a Sensei, or someone who has been training longer than you.

I have come to think of respect in a different way, that can be related to all involved in karate. I believe that the key message is to respect all around you, including yourself. Yes, I understand we are sensei to our students, but the critical part is that you must respect your students to the same level. We must all respect each other to the same degree.

As an example, I had a student named Robbie. We were doing a warm-up at the start of class and he needed me to roll up his pants as they were too big for him. As I did this, he began telling me a story about his day. I listened while I was helping him, and I gave him my full attention. That was all fine, and then he jumped back in line with the rest of the students. Later, we were focusing on students performing in front of the group to help prepare them for their upcoming grading.

As the students were up performing their moves, Robbie decided he wanted to have a chat with the boy next to him. I asked him to stop talking as he was distracting the students that were performing their katas. He continued to talk, so I decided to have a discussion with him about what respect was, and I said something like this...' Robbie, at the start of class, when I was helping you with your pants, you were telling me about your day. At any point did I just look away and start talking to someone else? No, I listened and showed you respect. I'm asking you to show the same respect to the students that are up and performing, and they will do the same for you when it's your turn. We have to make sure we respect each other. I'll respect you when you perform, and that goes with everyone in the class. Respecting each other is very important in our class. Do you understand what I'm asking?' Robbie responded with a yes, and he began to change his behaviour. Yes, Robbie was five years old— ha-ha—but that proves the point that respect should be taught at all ages.

I'm not saying that this will change Robbie's life after one class, but it is the consistent messaging I have throughout all of my classes, all the time. The repetition helps develop a new thought pattern for students, and the messaging works with all the principles that we want to teach our students.

This also applies to me as an instructor. If I'm talking, then I expect students to show respect and listen to me. If they're talking, it's my turn to show them the respect they deserve. We need to be the role models to our students and show them the way forward.

Principle #4 – Understanding the importance of being Consistent

This core principle is related to how an instructor teaches, but this does not necessarily mean we need to be discussing consistency as a concept with the students.

Having the same message consistently repeated over and over to the children is vital. We now provide a constant message regarding our three principles: Focus, Preparation, and Respect. The best way to explain the principles regularly is to describe how they work and why these principles are important.

You can use examples. For instance, if a student performs well at a grading, you can use that as a reference to having good preparation. If a student achieves a Focus stripe, we can use this as a reference to their positive development, and if a student shows great respect, we can use them as an example for all, showing the element of respect leading into becoming a role model in class.

These messages need to be given to the students over a long period until they become natural ways of being for them. It may seem repetitive on your behalf, but repetition is how you get a core message across to others. Over time, students understand that these principles represent your karate school, and the behaviours that are expected of students.

Conclusion

If a student walks through your doors and is given the opportunity to learn these core principles, I believe you will positively impact that student and help them to develop a strong sense of self-belief to become a better person than they were when they first walked in. That is our goal. We use karate as a tool to communicate with children, but our goal is to have a positive impact on their lives. That potential for them will give you a great sense of achievement. And this is why we're different from so many schools that see themselves as just teachers of karate.

· CORE PRINCIPLES ·
OF SUCCESS

#1 Strong FOCUS !

↓

#2 PREPARATION

↓

#3 RESPECT

↓

#4 CONSISTENCY

Kaizen Philosophy
(continuous development)

Kaizen Philosophy (continuous development)

At the age of sixteen, I had started my journey to becoming a world champion in kata for the World Karate Federation. In the following 15 years, while trying to become a world champion, I learned so much more that would develop into key life skills that led me to success in many areas of my life. Although this could be a whole chapter, I'd like to talk about Kaizen, the principle of Continuous Development, as it has had the greatest impact on my achievements in karate.

Kaizen is a mindset that can be used for everything. For example, I would train ten to twelve times per week and if I trained the same kata the same way every session, there is no doubt that I would have lost interest early on. Instead, each session, month, competition, world championship, I always looked to develop my kata by trying new methods. It is this pursuit of progression that keeps you motivated and engaged in what you're doing. When it comes to running a karate school, you will want to have a growth mindset and an attitude to become better, which will ensure you never become stale or unmotivated. If you lack continuous development, not only will you lose motivation, but you will also find that your competitors will pass you—the world doesn't wait for you to catch up. It's your job to stay one step ahead of everyone else and this will lead to your becoming successful in your desired goal.

I don't want you to look for big changes, as often it's the small things that count and that lead to achieving bigger goals and to creating a strong foundation for your karate school. This equals long term success.

KAIZEN

„CONTINUING IMPROVEMENT IN ALL
ASPECTS OF LIFE "

改善

KAI—CHANGE

ZEN—FOR THE BETTER

What needs to be constantly evaluated?

- Back-end processes: Our goal is to have supreme processes against others in our industry.

- Training programs to constantly develop and adapt our students and their needs: This includes how we teach, what we teach, the best ways to attract students, and the best ways to keep students.

Our goal is to continually develop all these factors to ensure all-round development across the whole business. If everyone in the company has this philosophy, there is no saying how large we can become and to owning a strong market share.

You can see that as instructors, we live the motto of Kaizen and we pass this skill onto our students to help them learn how to achieve goals in their lives.

We all need to maintain our passion, and continuous development is the key.

Building rapport and creating a community

When I first opened my karate school, I had a plan for teaching, a plan for marketing, a plan for growth, and I was ready to work hard. I thought that was all I needed, and over the first couple of years I learned some valuable lessons. One of these was that students can love the classes and the classes can run perfectly *but* unless the parents know what you're teaching their children or more importantly *why* you are teaching kata or kumite, then things can go awry. Fun is not enough to engage all your customers, which includes the parents. This might appear to be easier said than done, but if you are aware of this factor, then I am able to provide some steps to follow to ensure connection between everyone in the school.

I will cover the five components of building trust with your customers and provide you with an understanding of why they are crucial. If you follow these steps, you will build great relationships with everyone you come in contact with, and create an environment in which everyone feels comfortable.

We will cover the three stages of communication for you to follow, each based on where your school is at in its growth.

Five components of building TRUST

Trust is one of the most important ingredients in running a karate school and you will want to achieve a high level of trust with everyone from students to parents. There are four categories that we will assess to ensure you build a strong sense of trust with your customers. Often, we are doing well at two or three but not all four components, and all it takes is for one component to be missing to have an effect upon your relationship with your customers, that is to say, both students and parents.

#1 Competency

Competency is being good at what you do. Whatever service you provide, make sure it works and it helps people to develop. I know my program works as I have proven results, but it's important that the students and parents see this from their perspective. When a parent walks through the door for the first time, they don't know everything that goes into your karate school, they just see the results that appear in front of them with their child's development. Our job is to show that we can connect with our students, to motivate and inspire them through their training.

The first element that students and parents will use to start understanding how good our service is, will be when their child attempts their first belt. We have a grading day where students are tested, where they must come forward and perform their skills in front of their peers and parents. It's at this point that parents will see their child's great progression. This will translate to the parents and student having trust in you as an instructor and knowing that you are good at what you do. Amazing results will be seen, and that's the best part about karate, as it provides opportunities for everybody to stop and appreciate how much they've developed. In these gradings, parents may see developments in their children such as karate skills, focus, respect or confidence. It varies for each child as they all have different needs and they develop at different rates, but it will be at these evaluation opportunities where parents will feel that their children are in good hands.

#2 Inclusivity

People like to feel they are important and that they are a part of a community. It is critical to ensure we make our students and parents feel that inclusivity and this comes from how we communicate our messages to them. We can let students know what we're doing through classes and throughout the term, to give them a heads up and understand the direction of their training and the reasoning behind it. We explain why we perform certain exercises so they can understand the relationship to the development.

Communication with parents is crucial also, as they play a large role in the success of a karate school. One thing we learned in the first few years of our school was that while students felt inclusive, we failed to communicate adequately with the parents. Parents didn't know

100% about our program and how it worked. We assumed they did. Never assume!

Communication doesn't need to be complicated. It can be a simple chat with a parent about how our classes are run and how their child is progressing on their journey to becoming a black belt. This needs to be done consistently. We now chat with each person once a term to keep that relationship going. This is important because you want the parents to become enthusiastic fans as they're the ones who spread the word about how much their child loves karate.

#3 Disclosure

What is disclosure? It is being honest with students and parents about who you are and what you are doing, and why. A good example of great disclosure came when we decided to move seventy per cent of our students to a new location that was further away. The new dojo was better equipped, but unfortunately it's a fact that people don't like change.

We had the option to come up with an excuse to make it easier for us, but instead, we chose to be honest and to speak to every parent. Firstly, we sent a letter to everyone stating why we were moving, and we addressed potential FAQs they may have. Following that, we had one-on-one chats and answered any questions. We knew we risked losing a lot of students, but we knew that if we were honest, we wouldn't be caught out on anything, and then we would continue to build trust with them over time. We showed our vulnerability and it was up to them in the end. Ironically, we had a great response and overall great support. Yes, some students left, but we felt that by being honest and upfront, our customers respected us in return. I call this being transparent with people.

#4 Transparency

Being transparent is so important. If a student is falling behind, we don't sugar coat it, we set them small goals and if they're ready to go for their new belt, then they proceed. If not, that's okay, we will push for the next term's grading. I make this a strong point with all my students from day one. Students need to learn that in life not everything works perfectly and all you can do is do your best and the results will ultimately come. We are completely transparent throughout the whole term as to where a student is in their development. We answer questions such as Are they ready to grade? What do they need to fix? Do they need to set personal goals? Have they developed this term?

We have a consistent message for students and parents, so that all are aware of our training philosophy. This transparency creates strong trust in your relationships with students and with parents.

#5 Authenticity

Authenticity through conflict: You'll have times where a parent may contact you, perhaps in relation to why their child isn't being promoted for grading, or why you are running the classes the way you are. On such occasions you must be totally honest and explain why you do what you do. They may not agree, but they will respect you for your honest explanation. Again, you don't need to sugar coat anything, you should just be your authentic self.

BUILDING A COMMUNITY SPIRIT

3 Stages of communication

Stage 1: The instructor will write up a monthly report (*paragraph*) providing an opportunity to talk about how the students are going and the direction of each class. Parents love to hear from you, and this sets a form of communication to them as it will be difficult initially to do so while teaching classes. This will then be emailed to all customers via head office.

Stage 2: We have implemented our Leadership Program over a couple of years and have developed instructors through our Junior-Instructor Program. This will allow one class per term whereby you can spend time with parents and students discussing their development. This continues to build upon the relationship between instructor and customers. Here you can take on positive or negative feedback to ensure people feel listened to, the goal being always to improve your service to customers.

Stage 3: Select three parents to be a part of a social committee, which will be a mechanism for you to catch up for coffee and listen to ideas and feedback. These members will help drive your message to the other parents, and if you are unavailable to talk to parents, the committee members can answer questions on your behalf. This committee is your conduit to all your customers. You will still continue to have one-on-one conversations, but this committee will help you develop a community you will be looking to build.

Conclusion

We now have an understanding of some basic principles to follow through our five components of trust and we then connect them to our three forms of communication. These forms of communication will be set up in your class structure, so you need not stress about remembering them at the outset.

Developing new students *(step by step)*

A potential student walks through your doors and they attend a trial...

STEP 1 *(Evaluation of personality)*

Have a chat with the child and evaluate their personality. This will dictate how you run the trial. Of course, the practical part of the trial program will be the same, but the way you communicate this program may change from child to child, based upon individual personality types. You should be evaluating what the child likes and dislikes, for example, do they enjoy being loud and have high energy, or are they shy and prefer you to take a slow and gentle approach to training. The goal will be to make them feel comfortable and to build trust.

STEP 2 *(Run the Activity)*

Run the activity for the trial. They will decide whether they love it or not. This is their decision to make. Please remember that karate isn't for everyone, so don't take offense if it's not for them.

STEP 3 *(Create a connection)*

Your new student now joins your classes and I recommend at this point partnering them with a leader in the class or a role model student. Having a new friend in class will make them feel comfortable at the outset. In the first two weeks you don't want to be too hard on them, as this is the *hook* period. They need to have heaps of fun and not stress too much about being technically perfect. We still need to get them over the line, but now it's all about getting them to feel more comfortable as each class passes. Here we also evaluate how quickly they pick things up. This will help us know how much we can push them, and how easily they grasp things for their future development.

STEP 4 *(Implement the rules)*

Now they've had heaps of fun, they love coming to class and we can start to implement any rules they may need to know. For example, Billy was a new student who kept talking while I was giving out instructions, so acting immediately was the right time to start telling Billy our rules and expectations. This should not be delivered in a negative way, but in an informative way. I knew that if I enforced the rules too aggressively, there was a chance he might quit. In this particular case, over the next three to four weeks I implemented the rules more aggressively and eventually implemented consequences for bad behaviour. Yes, Billy learned over time, and although not perfect, we have seen a great improvement in his focus and respect and he is still enjoying karate.

STEP 5 *(Develop Focus)*

Now we teach the student how to have strong focus, as this will help them get to their next belt. Once they learn great focus, it is generally the case that teaching them the technical part becomes easy.

HAVING A STRONG FOCUS
IS THE KEY TO ACHIEVING GOALS

Three Elements of Focus

There are three elements in focus: *Creating a state of concentration *Performing specific tasks while in this state of concentration and *Creating a focused vision. (This is discussed in more detail in Chapter 4: Principle #1 – Establishing a strong Focus.)

One of my students, five-year-old Jarrod, is a perfect example for this step. When Jarrod started training with us, he loved coming to class. He was very young so we took the slow approach with his technical development. Then it came time to develop his focus. I had a chat with him and discussed what he needed to be able to do to achieve his next belt. I explained that he could be really good once he learned how to have strong focus and that I was about to teach him that. I said, 'Pick a spot on the wall and focus on that one spot'. I did it myself and showed him what that focus looked like, and I told him about how not becoming distracted is the goal. Then it was his turn, so I asked him to pick a spot on the wall and have a strong focus. I played a game to see if I could distract him... he won! High five!

Next, I wanted to develop moving focus. Jarrod jumped into the ready position with amazing focus and then I asked him to perform a block. He did three or four and they were okay. I explained to him, 'When you're in focus position doing a block, I want you to think about your hand and in moving it super-fast. If I think about being fast, then I will become super-fast.' Again I showed him an example and inspired him with speed. Then it was Jarrod's turn so I kept reminding him, 'Good focus and fast block'. I played a game with him, where we both performed the movement to see who was the fastest... Jarrod won! At that point I showed my excitement about how great he was and I made him feel amazing. He knew then what I was looking for, and how to be good at karate.

(Note: When counting a technique for a student, please remember the simple rule: if you count slow and soft, they will perform slow and soft. So, remember to count with confidence: loud and fast!)

The last stage of focus is in creating a focused vision. This is the vision to achieving his next belt and what he needs to do to get there.

Jarrod was then ready for his journey to a black belt.

Building leaders
in your school

Leadership is the backbone of a karate school. It will provide role models for other students and help support the growth of the school. I found that children aspire to become leaders and love to have the opportunity to do so.

What defines a leader?

Many factors make a good leader, but I like to focus on students becoming role models for good behaviour and good choices. This may include their listening skill, and the development of their technical skills, but also leading the way in how to behave in class.

It's best to communicate this message from day one of a student's journey.

In every class we pick captains to be at the front of a grouped line. When we select captains I will say, 'Who wants to be captain? Show me strong focus!' Students who follow these instructions and show strong focus and concentration are then selected for roles of responsibility. As you can see, they now begin to understand that if they show good choices in their behaviour, they will be rewarded. We do this also when new students join. We choose an established student to be a leader who will partner up with a new student to ensure they feel comfortable in their first class.

You may be surprised at how much children want to be more involved and to be given responsibility.

Over time, our definition of what makes a good leader was recognised, and informed one of the best programs we've ever implemented to date: The Leadership Program. We selected 15 students across the school who showed role modelling behaviours and we gave them the opportunity to become *Official Leaders*. They received a badge and were allocated a class during the week to attend, to help out other students. They were to become our apprentices and we would teach them how to communicate with other students and inspire them. This wasn't about gaining help for us in class, it's much more.

We are teaching these leaders to develop their leadership skills to the next level. Often, for the first six months, they watch, and I explain to them why I do certain things in class and I explain how they can do it. It's a long process, but every leader we have had has found this program to be one of the best elements they love about karate, and parents appreciate how we are giving back to the students in the school. Now we have children applying to be a part of the program and have created what I call dynamic fans of our karate school.

YOUNG STUDENTS BECOMING ROLE MODELS

Ultimately, you will find that this role modelling behaviour becomes ingrained in your culture. Do you remember the boy in the earlier chapter, shy Alex?

Alex had stopped coming for a term and then he decided to come back. We knew his karate was quite good, but he was really shy. As he joined the mat, he was clearly hesitant to jump back into class because he was nervous. I spoke to one of my other students, nine-year-old Vincent, and I explained the situation to him—that Alex was nervous about returning—and I asked Vincent to be a role model and have a chat with Alex to make him feel comfortable. Vincent did so without hesitation, demonstrating that another important element of good leadership is wanting to help others.

This program is about mentoring students to become mentors themselves. You will see these students develop into amazing instructors, possibly better than you were at that age. It will take time to develop the leadership program as initially you will have all beginners, but after one-and-a-half to-two years, you will be able to begin the selection process.

Conflict management

There is one thing you can't avoid and that's conflict. This is due to the simple fact that there will always be someone who complains about something. These issues can be difficult to handle, but there are some different scenarios I have learned from to ensure a positive outcome.

Parent Conflict

Scenario 1: First and foremost, it's so important to understand *why* you do everything you do. For example, whenever I make a decision—rightly or wrongly—I always base it on what I believe is in the best interests of the students. When it's time to discuss these decisions with a parent, I feel comfortable, as I am being honest and authentic with everything I do. When you make decisions for the wrong reasons, for example, based on money, that's where things can become difficult.

Scenario 2: If a parent comes to you during class and is creating conflict, *never* have that discussion there and then. You will have students waiting and you'll feel a sense of pressure to respond quickly, and you may not respond appropriately. As you have been put on the spot, you are unlikely to be able to make a calm and calculated response. Also, you should never have a negative discussion in front of other parents as they may start to discuss it with each other. In the worst case, if someone starts a conflict, take them aside and be very clear that you want to listen to what they have to say, but you have a class now, so you will call them the next day to resolve the issue. This will allow you to be prepared, to be calm, and to respond in the best way possible. You will then know what's coming, and you can implement a strategy for your discussion.

Scenario 3: Make the call to the parent, stay calm and never become the aggressor. When you phone, it's so important to listen first, and respond second. Allow them to get everything off their chest, and while they're talking, you can start to think about your response. Often, it may have been a matter of communication, as they may not know the reason behind a decision you have taken. The great thing is, every decision you have made has been in the best interests of the students. Right now, you need to be honest and authentic. I'm not saying they will agree with everything you say, but at the very least they will understand why you are doing something in a particular way. There is a point where you may politely draw the line and they either accept your decision, or maybe your school isn't for them. Over the first couple of years, you will find that you'll need to filter out the customers that are never going to be happy, from those who are your enthusiastic fans. You're better off with fewer students who love the service you provide.

Student Conflict

If there is a conflict with a student, the way you handle the situation will be based on the type of personality they have.

Let's use some examples and talk about how we handle each situation.

Student Example 1

Situation: A student has broken a rule and after many warnings, you send them to the naughty mat for a couple of minutes, at which point, they start to cry.

Resolution: Go to the child and have a chat. Remain calm and don't freak out just because they are crying, as there should be no reason for it, but they do need to understand about consequences. I would explain to them what happened, and how it was distracting others, and I would talk about how I know that they usually make good choices in their behaviour. I would then set goals and lead them back into class. This can be done over and over until behaviour changes. At the end of class, I would speak to the child's parents and keep them informed about what was said and where their child is at in regard to their karate development. If the child decides to run off to their parents or not listen, there's nothing you can do at this stage besides giving them the option to jump back into class when they are ready.

One really important piece of advice I use to all students: 'It's okay to make mistakes. We understand that everyone makes mistakes. You are not in trouble, but we don't want you to make the same mistake twice—we want to learn from our mistakes'.

Student Example 2

Situation: The student shuts down on all communication with you and refuses to listen or do any training. They may sit down and zone out.

Resolution: When you know that no matter what you say, the student won't listen, let them be, give them the option to join in when they want to, and be sure to let them know that they are more than welcome when they're ready. You can't force a child to continue your class when they are not willing. Make it a priority to talk after class to a parent or give them a call to discuss the situation.

Conclusion

Most conflicts with students arise from them not following the rules or failing to communicate with you. I always treat them as an adult, I ask their thoughts on the issue, listen and show respect and in return I calmly explain why a rule is a rule, and they generally understand. When children are given logical reasons and explanations as to why expectations have been set, they will usually follow instructions as they will see there is a purpose and reason. At times, students may also misbehave because the rules were simply unclear to them. Once you make these clear, you can continue to have high expectations of your students. There should be no reason for any conflicts to escalate. If a student continues to break rules, then it's important to discuss this with their parent and discuss steps to move forward.

The importance of class evaluation

A successful business is one that constantly evaluates its performance and continually improves its service to customers. That's what I did for the first six years and it is what I continue to do at my karate school. The moment we think we know it all is the moment we are likely to fall behind.

Performance evaluation doesn't need to be complicated, it's a matter of following two forms of assessment.

Step One is to reflect as a general overview at the end of a night of teaching about how you felt it went and where you had difficulties that you might improve on next time. It's like training for a world championship: you don't do the same thing all the time, you try and better each technique in kata, and that never ends. You'll find the more you do this, the better an instructor you will become. Your confidence will build, and teaching will become an effortless task.

Step Two is to reflect at the end of each term about what worked and what didn't, in respect of the general program. We should ask questions such as: Did we do too much kata and not enough kumite? Were the students tired by the end of the term? If so, why? etc.

A good program has great flow throughout the year and adjusts to the students' needs as the year proceeds. The goal is for students to get to the end of the year filled with excitement, and pumped for the next year to come, rather than being exhausted from a long year.

An example of changing and developing a program:

I had a class of twenty students and I was running it as one big group, comprised of five new students and another five white belts, and the other ten students were all junior orange belts. It was so much work to control all the students and to maintain their focus. I evaluated what could be done better on our end and felt we could divide into two smaller groups. One group of white belts would play a game with the Junior-instructor (as they weren't technically good enough to teach techniques) and I would do basics/kata with the orange belts. Then at the halfway mark, we would have a break and swap groups. I then got the white belts and orange belts to play fun games. This structure worked a treat. Everyone had good focus, they were well controlled, and I didn't feel exhausted by the end of a class: all accomplished with just a few small changes.

This was one example of a logistics strategy and there will be several similar things that can be adopted in class, depending on the students participating—it's a matter of adapting as you go.

Conclusion

When starting a new school, you will go through many different stages of development. Structure changes when:

- numbers fluctuate in class
- there are varied levels of development (belts)
- there are different personalities of students that effects how they work together

You manage what you have in front of you and go from there. At my school, I have gone through all the stages and now know what needs to be done and when. This took a lot of trial and error but now I have a karate program that runs effortlessly.

Students: Personality types

Students: Personality types

It is important to understand the different types of personalities that will walk through the doors and that your communication style may need to adjust to in order to get the most out of a student. Firstly, you need to understand that karate isn't for every child, and that your job is to provide the best service possible. However, knowing all that, karate may still not be for some. Don't take it personally if someone doesn't like karate or ends up leaving, but take solace in the fact that you are providing the best service you can provide. It's up to the student in the end, and there could be external factors that affect their decision-making that you may not be aware of.

When a student first walks through the doors, you will need to evaluate their skill set in karate, and more importantly, evaluate their personality. This will help you as an instructor to understand the best method of communication for each student.

I always recommend that you be yourself and be open with each student. Be honest about how you teach, and they will respect you and in turn open up to you as their instructor. This will start building rapport.

By building rapport, you can more easily evaluate some simple patterns in a person that will allow you to adjust your communication style and help them feel more comfortable around you. For example, some children don't like to stand too close when talking to you, or they may not enjoy having any contact with you when you're chatting with them, such as placing your hand on their shoulder.

Others may have high energy and get a lot closer when talking with you and may be excited to give you a high five. It doesn't take long to figure it out, and it's your job to evaluate a student's communication style and adjust to it so they begin to feel a sense of comfort around you.

From there, we start setting goals. Once we've gained trust and they understand the rules, they can start their karate journey.

Types of students that will walk through your doors:

The Shy Student

A well behaved student who is good at karate, but lacks the confidence to show their full potential. Needing only a gentle push at the start, as you're still building trust with them. Let them make their own pace, and focus on the small goals they are achieving. It doesn't have to be at every session, but when they achieve a small goal, make sure they know how well they have done. Often, when a child has a low sense of confidence, they can't see the progression in their development, so it becomes the job of the instructor to ensure the message is getting through that they are moving forward and achieving goals. Everyone feels good when they are progressing, and this goes for children as well as for adults.

If you have a student who is super-shy or nervous about joining in, I often get them to sit on the side of the mat and give them the option to join when they feel comfortable. The golden rule is that you must not force a child to do something they don't want to do, you can only give them the option in a friendly manner, and the rest is up to them.

Another strategy is to team up a shy student with a role model in a class. This will provide a sense of friendship and comfort and a sense that they are not alone. This will help Alex and it will also help the role model child become a better leader as they have been given responsibility to help out.

The Overconfident Student

A great student, very respectful and listens to all instructions given. With the determination to succeed and is willing to do extra hard yards to achieve their goals. By no means is this seen as a negative, in fact, we love this about them. But we do know there will be a point at which their confidence will create a hurdle for themselves in progressing forward. They like to be pushed, specifically at things they are good at. In the early stages of karate it's not complicated, and they find it easy and love to be pushed and enjoys progressing faster than most students.

Eventually, I knew they would hit a hurdle. Up until then, they pick up the teachings quite easily and then, for the first time, was put to the test. They may have to learn a technical stance— ie. the kat stance, one of the hardest stances for students to learn, but so critical to their progression.

They find it hard to adapt, and struggle to perfect this stance. What you would generally see with the *overconfident student* is 100% effort, but when they don't get it right, they become very frustrated, as they can be perfectionists. They can become disheartened through this period, so it is important for the instructor to adopt a different style of communication at that point. We don't push them, because now failure had entered their thinking process, which isn't a bad thing on the whole, as everyone needs to learn how to deal with failure at some point. However, I slow down the process, lowered the expectations and ensure they don't put pressure on themselves. I would now break down the technique and give them small goals to achieve throughout the process.

I stated earlier on in the book that humans feel good as long as they are progressing, no matter how slow or fast, they just need to see a progression. We use the same philosophy with our students: they need small goals to achieve that feeling of progression to create a consistent stream of development.

If we don't help the *overconfident student* through this period, they will become frustrated and not enjoy training anymore and I wouldn't blame them... why train when you're not having fun!

The Uncoordinated Student

I still remember when a student by the name of Tommy first walked through our doors. We had a simple coordination exercise for the students, which was for them to adopt our kumite stance and start hopping on the spot, then slowly moving forward. Tommy was unable to bounce on two feet and to land at the same time, and I could see that Tommy would need resilience and commitment to be able to progress. Like all sports, karate is based on coordination, and at times, with stances and techniques, it can be very unnatural for the human body.

With highly uncoordinated students, you need to explain the slow process, the importance of patience, and not to compare oneself to others. If they can do this, they will achieve big goals.

I needed to show Tommy that I was patient and that I believed in him. It's at this point you start to develop a relationship built upon trust between instructor and student.

We took it step by step until we started to see progress. It was important that I spoke with Tommy and showed him the progress he had made and the goals he had achieved. I built it up to be something special, to help instil a sense of self-belief for him.

We used this same process over and over for all of his set goals and I am proud to say that after six years, Tommy was still training with us and had developed in leaps and bounds over that time. He had something special: patience and determination, and I reminded him regularly that it was this skill set that he could use in any part of his life to achieve a goal.

The Quiet Student

At first these students can be very reserved. An element here is that they may be feeling uncomfortable around you.

You may have high energy towards students in your classes, and you don't want to stop that for one student. As you can see, running up to a *quiet student* screaming, 'Give me a high five! Woohoo' may be overwhelming. Instead, first evaluate their responses to your behaviour. You can still have that natural high energy in the class but when you look to communicate with them directly, you drop the tone, slow it down and communicate at a level where they feel comfortable.

You should do this for the first few weeks. It's important that you stay true to yourself and they see who you genuinely are as a person. Over time, they will start to adapt to your high energy and start to feel more comfortable with you. Then, you can start to raise your energy when communicating directly with them. You'll see from time-to-time that they will give you a cheeky smile and eventually be comfortable around you. That will be the time that you can go for the high five and have a laugh. This is how you help them build their confidence in the early stages. You'd be surprised how often a student walks through the door and you're able to get the best out of them. Again, the priority is to gain trust from the student and then the doors will open to help them even more.

The Student with a Learning difficulty

You'll find that students with learning difficulties find it hard to communicate with you when you're trying to talk with them. They may struggle to focus and to listen to basic instructions. One way I have been able to tell if a student has trouble communicating is through eye contact. It is usually difficult to make eye contact with them at all. Children with learning difficulties will need you to remain calm and you will need to understand that comprehending some messages is going to be a challenge for them. Please remember that you can only do the best you can. This is why it's important to provide a free trial to a potential student, to see if they will benefit from participating in your classes. If staying still and following basic instructions is challenging, they may need more of a one-on-one approach than being in a group class. Sometimes, these children simply need a little bit more time to mature before starting a sport. We don't want to waste parents' money or time if their child participates in our classes but is not gaining any benefits from it. There isn't much we can do if focus is not possible for a child, however, in saying this, we have had many students with learning difficulties who have had successful results.

Students with learning difficulties benefit from clear rules and boundaries in your class, for instance, in listening when an instructor is talking. We look to build a relationship, so if there comes a time when we need to enforce a rule and consequence, we can do so without creating too much of a negative impact on the child. It is important to stay persistent when it comes to students and the rules, as structure helps them to manage on a day-to-day basis.

There will come a time that like everyone else, all students will need to follow the rules or else face the consequences, such as missing out on parts of the class. They may have been given three warnings to stop talking and on the fourth time, you send them to the naughty mat, and they miss out on game time. Of course, at this point, you explain why they missed out and what they need to do to avoid being in trouble again. You also show the student that you believe they can demonstrate good behaviour, but this doesn't mean that they're exempt from the consequences of not abiding by the rules. They will then begin to learn to adapt and follow instructions— positive development—or they may also choose to quit the class. All you can do is ensure a positive environment and structure for them to develop. Often it does, and sometimes it doesn't, but we need to understand that there is a class of fifteen students all of whom are important, and we can't therefore solely focus on one student all the time as this affects the development of the students making up the majority of the class.

A possible scenario:

The student comes to class and decides to run around the other side of the hall and not listen to anything you say. You must understand that they may have difficulty with communication skills and there's nothing you can do about that. You ask them to join the class a couple of times but with no response. At this stage you should let them do their thing and you should try to talk with their parents after class and explain that for a child to participate in class they need to follow basic instructions. If this is not achievable, at this point it's better for the student to take some time off and allow them to mature and try again in another six months or so and re-evaluate the situation then.

The Born Leader Student

There are some students in whom you want to develop leadership skills and then there are the *Born Leaders* of the world who were born with leadership skills. Once I recognised this in a student, I look to take those skills to the next level. Although they may be a natural, there are levels of leadership, and it was my job to help them develop these skills at an appropriate pace.

They seem to learn quickly, and soon become very comfortable. When I see them at a comfort level, I placed them in a more advanced position, such as leading a warm-up and basic session, even if they feel they aren't ready.

To develop this student I need them to understand that development sometimes means pushing your limits and sometimes feeling vulnerable. It's easy to forget to push someone like this, as it can sometimes be easier to let them do what they are doing as it becomes so effortless for all.

Leaders are a large part of your school's development. They become role models at the school and sometimes future instructors, so make sure you invest time in their development.

What defines a Leader?

In our school, becoming a leader equals becoming a role model, a person who models the behaviour we want to develop in our students. That behaviour may be a demonstration of great focus, or of great respect, or we might see that leadership behaviour in someone who likes to help others. The requirements to be a leader change, depending on the individual student. It may not be the contributions made during class, but more about the behaviours displayed throughout the class. The goal is for students to look at a leader and say, 'I want to be like them and that is the behaviour I need to develop in order to achieve their level'.

The next stage in the development of a leader is to teach them how to communicate with other students, young and old. It's a slow process, but done with patience, we can teach our leaders the different ways of communication with others.

The never give up attitude Student

Samantha comes into class and gives it everything she's got. She struggles at the start to get going so it's important through this period that I keep encouraging her through her challenges. All I ask from a student is that they give it their best and if they do, then I know they will achieve big goals. When karate seems particularly challenging for a student, they can take the easy way out and quit, so those who stay and push through should be respected for their actions, as this is an amazing quality to have as a child.

I told Samantha to never give up and if she continued to train hard, it would turn around and she would become great at karate and that's exactly what happened.

Samantha had a brother, ironically he was an *overconfident student*. Samantha was always behind him and felt like she was the under-achiever of the two, but she didn't let it affect her, instead, she used this to push herself even more. She's six years old, so it's amazing what kids can do and the character they have at such a young age. Like every student, she will have her ups and downs and we will be there for her during those periods. It's important to understand her personality so we can communicate on her level when needed.

The talker Student

With Ricky, I knew the biggest rule he would struggle to follow was not to talk when others (me) are talking and to respect others throughout the class. Before I told him this specific rule, I made sure I followed the same rule—when he was talking, I listened and didn't interrupt. Then I could ask for the same respect in return.

When you enforce rules, you need to remember that all in the class are equal and that includes you as the teacher. As instructors, we need to role model our expectations.

After telling Ricky this rule, I started to enforce it and set boundaries for him. Often, I found that he would talk and socialise with others, and while socialising is positive, it started to become a distraction to other students.

It was time to enforce the rules with Ricky and the consequences that came with them. I gave him a clear understanding of what would happen if he didn't follow the rules. When he did not respect others, he spent time out of the class on the naughty mat and I would explain to him why he was in that position and that I believed he had it in him to turn things around.

I always make it very clear to students that there is a line. When it's time to have fun, they can make noise and enjoy themselves, but when I'm teaching, I expect them to respect me and to listen. You must be very clear on your expectations of how the class will be run.

I spoke to Ricky about becoming a role model in class and becoming someone with great behaviour. It didn't happen overnight, but at least every time he was in trouble, he wasn't upset with me, rather looking at how he could improve. This happened for a couple of years, but I can tell you that yes, he became a role model, and one of our best students in the class, demonstrating amazing respect and focus.

I want you to see Ricky through my eyes: he goes to school; he loves to engage with others but constantly gets told off and told that he is the naughty one—it's our job to believe in him.

Sometimes the Rickys' will quit, but sometimes you can get through to Ricky and that's our long-term goal, to have an impact on children's lives.

Student: Little Bobby — cute, but doesn't listen to a word you say

Bobby is that little student who comes in, so cute, and he talks like a chipmunk, and you just want to cuddle him... Hmm, but the problem is, he doesn't listen to a word you say, yet finds a way to make you laugh. This is a tough one... you want to make sure the rules are enforced but the simple fact is that sometimes you need to swallow your pride and chill out. I found that with Bobby I had to allow him to go at his own pace.

It took a long time to build trust with him and often he'd cry if I told him off or even just explained the rules to him. He would run out of class to his mum and I just had to let him go. Over time, I started to enforce the rules more and more as I built trust with him. He started to listen, and by the time he was six years old, he was one of the best students in his class. It had taken a very long time for Bobby to progress through his belts, but being patient was the best thing for him.

Every child is different and that's why we need to evaluate a student's personality, to ensure we communicate with them in the best possible way for them.

UNDERSTANDING
WHO OUR STUDENTS
ARE IS THE KEY

Conclusion

As you have seen, there are many different types of personalities that walk into a karate school. The best service you can render is in understanding how to communicate with each student to get the best out of them.

It may sound a bit complicated, this need to evaluate each person, but once you're working in a class it means you won't be needing to spend twenty minutes with each student, which would be exhausting.

You will run each class as a group and in the way you feel most comfortable. When talking to students individually, you adopt a communication style that helps them feel comfortable around you and that also builds a connection between student and instructor. This is done as one-liners said here and there, rather than long conversations. It will become a natural part of the teaching process that you'll develop over time.

As you can see, this is the best part of karate for students. They can socialise in group activities and at the same time develop their own personal needs.

Gradings and why they are so important to a karate school

Gradings are the backbone of a karate school. The fact is, a student joins karate to become black belt, and gradings provide the journey to the destination. You'll see students at times lack motivation and then go for their next belt, which becomes a motivation booster.

Without grading, students would train and find it difficult to see improvement in themselves on a regular basis. A grading gives everyone, including students, parents and instructors, a time to stop and appreciate the progress of a student. You'll find you will love gradings, as it will offer a sense of fulfilment as you observe your students' progress through their stages.

Through grading, we can teach so many lessons to our students:

- If you want to achieve a big goal, you must set a vision (black belt) and then set small goals to achieve along the way (kyu grades). This will translate to any goal a child may have in their life.

- We only send a student to a grading if they are at their personal best... we don't give belts away simply to keep students happy. This teaches them that if they want to be successful, they will need to put in the hard work and not expect a free ride.

- If a student isn't ready to grade, they may be very disappointed, but this teaches them to be persistent and not to give up. We must all deal with disappointment at some point in our lives. Resilience is key here and in working out a plan to achieve a goal.

- Sometimes, a student isn't ready to grade but they decide to put in extra effort and train at home, the rule being: if you're ready we will send you. This teaches them that if they are willing to put in the extra hard work, they will have the chance to achieve any goal they set their hearts on.

- We prepare for gradings in the weeks beforehand, with the messaging to students that if you want to perform well, you need to prepare for it so you are more than ready on the day. This support will help them get over any anxiety or nerves.

Sending students to grading: This subject is so important, as it represents what you stand for as a karate school. You need to keep in mind that every student is different and progress should be judged in line with their ability.

Sending a student to a grading early as a mechanism to keeping them or their family happy does not offer a child any opportunities to learn or to develop. That would not send a positive message for what we stand for. We always take notes on a student's technical development, and what they need to work on. This helps when having an honest conversation with students and their parents as to whether students are ready to grade or not. Sending them early will only make it more difficult for the student at their next belt, as each belt syllabus is set up to help the student in their next belt requirements. It's important to achieve all the requirements to the best of their ability.

All of these points become a unique selling point to parents when they are looking for their child to start a sport. Karate offers much more than just sporting ability—it develops life skills.

To finish off this chapter I will leave you with a message I received from a parent about their children who train with us. This exemplifies our goal as instructors, and the grading process that plays such a large part in success.

GRADINGS-A CHANCE TO SEE THE PROGRESSION OF A STUDENTS JOURNEY

Dear James, I've just wanted to say how much I admire your team for their passion and dedication...you are certainly making a difference to the life of our boys. I am sure when our boys get more mature they too will appreciate more and more of your teaching.

I like the fact that you don't just show the kids karate techniques, you coach and guide them to become responsible, resilient and disciplined individuals. I am so glad that you've set up the school near our home and that we have been able to enrol all of our boys. Thank you!

Receiving feedback like this gives me a sense of achievement that I'm making a positive change in this world and having an impact on my students' lives. That's what it's all about. True happiness.

Developing future instructors

When first opening a karate school, the main priority is to set up a program and structure that creates fun and easy flowing classes, and that is based on one instructor running the classes. We will look to continuously improving our program and investing in becoming better instructors.

Once the school has settled and you have loyal students attending, it will then be time to begin the search for leaders amongst the students. These are students who will have shown leadership skills: caring for others, being role models, and having a passion for karate.

We developed a leadership program for these selected students. The program involves instructors mentoring students and developing their leadership skills. This includes how to communicate with other students and how to teach karate. Students love this extra responsibility. Although this is a slow process, it is a crucial one. We must be patient and take our time in developing these students as they are the future of the school.

We allocate one class per week for rising leaders to develop new skills. This can start from the age of 9, depending on the student's maturity. Although every school is different, this program is best introduced after the school has been running for a year or two. This will give you time to develop these students to the level you require. Such a trainee may be a leader for a couple of years before they may be hired for casual work. When they turn fifteen, we usually review where they're at and make the decision whether to provide them with a job opportunity.

Hiring someone to become a junior instructor is an important decision and it is crucial you select the right person for the job, as you will eventually lean on them throughout the teaching process. Once they're hired, they will need mentoring, and they will continue to learn about teaching and how to become a better instructor. This will require a lot of patience from both sides. There are many phases we follow in developing an instructor and this is shown during my mentoring program with head instructors. I will discuss how to motivate students and how to get the best out of them during their time with you.

Whoever you hire must love karate and love training under your school. There would be no point investing all your time and energy into the wrong person to find that they leave at the end of their training. The elements we look for in instructors and leaders:

- They have a good karate skill set
- They like helping others
- They are role models within the class
- They have a passion for karate

Different Types of Instructors to look out for:

#1 - **The teen beginner**: This type of student starts in their teens, enjoys karate, is good but not perfect, a little shy, yet has a great attitude towards karate and our program. They show great trust in us as instructors, and are passionate in their training. They always listen, and take on board our instructions and are always respectful. We then sit down and pitch what it means to be an instructor at our school. We highlight that it's much more than just helping out in class, it is about the person they will become.

#2 - **The young beginner**: This type of student has been training for five years and started at around the age of ten years old. They always show confidence in class and always socialise with other students, they are constantly wanting to become better, and they ask questions about how to improve. Karate is their life, they are passionate and want to be a part of your school. They still have some work to do on their technical ability, but they give 110% in their training and have reached their brown belt. We anticipate it will be a long process for this person as it can take them some time to become familiar with new content. We implement a review process and give feedback on what needs to improve. We don't overload them, we simply want them to get the basics right.

#3 – The shy starter: This type of student was always really shy but demonstrated great technical ability, so we decide to give them a go. It might be a very slow process to get them out of their shell, but gradually they start to build their teaching skills and confidence. One trainee in this category that comes to mind demonstrated a *slow burn* process but eventually they became super confident and an amazing teacher who connected well with the students. I put this down to a willing attitude to learn and to becoming better (continuous improvement), with a great attitude towards training and teaching, and these elements ultimately made them a great teacher. There was a point in their development where we gave them more responsibility and they stepped up. This taught us that sometimes you have to take a chance and give someone the opportunity to show what they have. That person became one of our best instructors and this taught me not to judge a book by its cover. Again, attitude is everything!

Whichever category a junior instructor comes from, gradually, we would add more responsibility to the junior instructor's role. Occasionally, they might hesitate to take on the next stage due to a lack of belief in themselves. We continue to push step-by-step and show our belief in them throughout this period. Mentoring is what they need: someone to believe in and support them to reach the next level in karate and teaching.

Our structure for junior instructors isn't for them to run full classes but to help out in classes and take some of the pressure off the head instructor. We continue to keep an eye on them over the next year or so and with the need for us to make a decision as to whether or not they are up for the job, we give them every possible chance for success. Nobody is perfect, and everyone will have different weaknesses as teachers. The goal is to identify students who can mould and align their beliefs with your school.

General Tips to developing an Instructor:

It's important at first that the junior instructors understand the responsibilities of work, including being on time, following the rules, etc. They can easily mistake this job for just something fun at karate, and yes, it *is* fun, but it is also a job with responsibilities and this needs to be made clear.

First responsibilities should start with junior instructors running the stretch segment, as that's the easiest and best way to connect with students in a class. Over the following few weeks, the next goal will be to ensure students are behaving in class (listening when the instructor is talking, or lining up when asked), while at the same time, the junior instructor should begin to give positive feedback to students and begin to develop a rapport with students in their classes.

From there they can start to teach basic techniques to white belts, with no more than two to three students at a time. The junior instructor should be given clear instructions on how to teach techniques to the students, so that they develop the confidence and ability to teach.

Depending upon on their level of progression and maturity, responsibilities can be gradually increased.

You must constantly give junior-instructors feedback and not assume they know everything. It's important that you not only explain what to do but why you do it. This will give them confidence in knowing why they are teaching, and what they're teaching. When they do something well, give them positive feedback so they know they are developing. Set specific goals for the junior-instructors and build on from there, making sure you are clear in your instructions and requirements.

It's also important to teach junior-instructors how best to communicate with students, for example how we talk with a five-year-old is different to how we would talk with a twelve-year-old.

This will be a slow process but if done correctly, you will have smoothly running classes and you will find that pressure comes off the head instructor when you and the junior-instructor work as a team.

Process of developing karate Instructors:

1. Evaluate who in your classes shows leadership skill
2. Invite those students to join the Leadership Program
3. Evaluate if they would fit in as an instructor at your school
4. At fifteen years of age, offer a student a job

5. Give the magical pitch to them, so they are pumped to work for you

6. Make the rules of engagement clear, as they can think it's all just fun and not a real job

7. Continue to develop their skills and invest in them as students and instructors

8. Review progress

9. Decide if this is the right job for your selected candidate

PROCESS TO DEVELOP INSTRUCTORS

STAGE #1 EVALUATE STUDENTS SKILLSET

STAGE #2 EVALUATE THEIR RAPPORT WITH OTHERS

STAGE #3 ROLE MODELLING BEHAVIOUR

STAGE #4 PASSIONATE ABOUT KARATE

STAGE #5 CREATE A PROGRAM TO DEVELOP INSTRUCTORS SKILLS

Different karate styles and programs
(where do you fit in?)

As you would know, there are many styles of karate. The four major styles are Shito-Ryu, Goju-Ryu, Shotokan-Ryu and Wado-Ryu, as well as many offshoots from these styles.

Each style has its method of training, including different stances and techniques. The interesting thing is that they generally have similar katas in their syllabuses, but they may be performed in their own styles, for example, Heian Nidan, Sadan, Chodan are each performed in their particular way.

Is one style better than the other? There are positives and negatives in all styles, but without any ego, I believe it comes down to the individual instructor and how they teach their students. The more important questions are: Do they follow a specific program layout during classes, or do they teach as they go? Do they have processes to follow, and do they communicate well with students?

Over six years I considered our original Shito-Ryu syllabus and analysed its strengths and weaknesses, in an attempt to provide a better product for my students. What I found was that the syllabus was first created many years ago for Japanese students. One thing you will have noted if you've travelled to Japan, is that their culture is very different from our western culture. Karate is a lifestyle, a culture created hundreds of years ago. Japanese children train for hours a day, with karate embedded in their school curriculum as a school sport, and it is highly respected by the community. It's not about games and fun, it's about commitment, focus and development. Students don't question or critically think anything, and they show a high level of respect for their teachers.

I once went to train with my idol, Sakumoto Sensei in Okinawa. I went to his house one night for celebratory drinks, but beforehand we trained in his dojo downstairs. I was training for a world championship, and can I tell you, training in his general class, I struggled to keep up. Most students there weren't training for a world championship, they were just training as their daily routine. I took a photo with the class and felt that any one of those students around me could win a world championship, but that's not what it's all about for the Japanese, it's much more.

Years later, I looked back at that photo and I realised that the young student next to me was Ryo Kiyuna who became the world kata champion multiple times. My point is, karate is different in Japan, it isn't just a sport, it's embedded in their culture.

The western world is more relaxed—life is more about socialising, and our kids are doing three sports at the same time. Their focus is not at the same level as their Japanese counterparts and there are perhaps many more distractions that our children face. So why would we have the same syllabus as that for a Japanese child? That would be setting our kids up for failure.

From this reflection, we decided to keep the core of karate tradition in our syllabus but adapted it to our target demographic, which is Australian children. This allows us to teach the core aspects of karate and for students to enjoy themselves at the same time. We broke down the syllabus in specific areas where we had learned students needed more development. It's all about getting the best out of our students and having a high retention percentage. The longer you have a student, the more you can help them develop.

Where karate schools often fail to grow is in creating processes for people to follow. Our concept allows a school to provide better karate classes, and instead of winging it on the day, there is a plan in place to help students reach their desired destination.

A good teacher is one who can connect with every student in their class: knowing what to say and when to say it, how to motivate a student and how to communicate the pathway to black belt. Can you see that nothing in the above relates to style? **Karate is the tool we use to have a common interest with a student, allowing us to connect with them and teach the core aspects of karate including respect, focus, discipline... and the list goes on.**

Often people look at styles of karate as the be-all, and forget that the core part of karate is helping others. No ego! It's all about how to help a student develop. We leave egos at the door and this is a great message to pass on to your students.

Conclusion

Yes, there are many different styles. They all have similarities but, in the end, it's about the instructor and how they teach. I have found that being successful comes down to two things: One: Teaching for the right reasons; and Two: Being guided and having processes to follow so an instructor can enjoy their time teaching for many years to come.

Your style, your dojo.

Your dojo will be more than just what style you train, it's about how it runs, how you connect with your students, and teaching with a clear understanding of what works and what doesn't. Having superior processes in your business will ensure that your school will have a strong point of difference from other schools around you.

DIFFERENT STYLES WITH THE SAME GOAL

STYLE #1   STYLE #2

SAME GOAL
INSPIRING
STUDENTS

STYLE #3   STYLE #4

Adapting to Change
(revisiting Covid-19)

The year 2020 impacted small businesses around the world like never before, including ours. In this chapter I discuss how decision-making was tested and how we continued to overcome obstacles that came our way. Covid-19 became a perfect example of how best to analyse and to deal with difficult business decisions.

When I look at the decisions we made, it doesn't look like rocket science, but believe me, when the pressure hits and everything around you is crumbling, your back is against the wall, and you have big decisions to make. Either you let fear take over and cloud your judgment, or you stay calm, composed and don't stop strategising until you find the right answers to move forward.

It was the last two weeks of the school term and we were preparing for our end of term grading. As it happened, it was to be one of our largest gradings ever, with over 150 students attending.

While my business partner was overseas, our Prime Minister announced that anyone arriving back into Australia from travel abroad would need to quarantine for 14 days on arrival. Oh no!... there goes my business partner for the rest of the term. We knew that our school would have to close its doors, so the questions were: When? and, What do we do?

It was important to remember that every decision we make has to come from the right place, and in this case it was: What is best for our students and parents? and *not* How are we going to make money?

We started recording online classes over the next two weeks, every day recording for eight hours, and then teaching at night. Some people wondered why we were recording classes, as they thought we were not likely to need to close any time soon. In difficult times, it pays to be pro-active and to do whatever it takes to survive.

We were able to complete the final two weeks of the school term classes and we demonstrated to our parents that we were on high alert. We followed all regulations and rules established by the government, including limiting the number of people in a dojo at a given time, and we maintained social distancing with two square metres of space between students. We needed to ensure we maintained the trust of parents during this difficult time.

Then the final blow hit. We received the announcement that all karate schools would need to close for at least the next three months. What would we do?

Looking at all options, the one adopted by most other schools I had been in contact with, was to provide virtual classes live, via Zoom or Facebook. This idea sounded fresh and exciting but after close evaluation as to what would be best for our students, it was clear there was no easy solution. My deliberations included:

- Classes needed to be engaging for the usual 40-minute duration, and it would be difficult to actually help students during the classes as well as maintaining a high energy environment. It could work, but was it the best solution?

- I needed to avoid teacher burnout. Would back-to-back online classes exhaust teachers over an three month period?

- Would the school's survival for the long term be assured or was this a stop-gap solution for now? And how would the answer to that question impact our students?

- If turnout from students for virtual classes was low, would that translate to the participating students as a negative in their motivation? The numbers participating on any given occasion would be out of my control.

After evaluating our options, the question was: Is there another way?

In seeking an answer, I firstly re-evaluated our main objectives:

- students need to be engaged in all our classes over a long period

- high attendance is needed, in order to maximise student motivation, therefore, I need to create strong content

- student progression needs to be maintained – achieving goals at home just as at the dojo

- the development of our program for the future needs to be maintained

What would we do? ... We had a week to decide!

I brainstormed ideas with my head of website development and discussed an online portal that all students would have password access to. This by far outweighed all other ideas put forward, and with a lot of hard work and commitment, we could develop a portal that would add to our karate program for years to come.

There were actually several positive components to this idea:

1. In the event that you didn't already know, our karate website is ranked in Google for its SEO (Search Engine Optimisation). The higher we rank in SEO, the higher is the chance that a prospective customer will find our karate school in a Google search.

One element of this ranking system is the traffic that comes through to our website. By creating an online portal on our website, all our students would force traffic to our site instead of to Zoom or Facebook (and the latter would do nothing for our business). After nearly four months of running our online portal, we had over 10,000 views through our website. This is priceless SEO development, without spendin

2. We developed three different sections on our portal. One was Online Classes, uploaded twice a week and developed for six different age and belt groups. Our simplified class structure allowed us to run classes for the whole school of 280+ students, all in two nights of training per week. How good was that! A second section was a page dedicated to students' learning New Kata and Basics that they needed for their next belt grading. We recorded every belt level and discussed in detail what students needed to learn to be able to grade for their next belt. The results of this element were amazing, as we graded that term with 100+ students who were all more than ready to grade. The third section was a Virtual Sensei Live Chat whereby every fortnight we ran a live discussion board from our website to catch up with our students and connect with them as a group. This was a great success, as all our students love a chat. ☺

3. In a live feed, you don't have control of quality, and most importantly, the energy of the class. By pre-recording, I could edit the videos, have game segments placed into the classes, and ensure that it was a full class of high energy training. It was simple... if something didn't work, I would edit it

out. It was a lot of work for hundreds of videos but you do whatever it takes to achieve the best outcome.

4. When we returned to actual classes, we maintained our online portal to more fully support our students in the rest of their karate journey. If students want to do extra training at home now, they have the tools to help them for years to come. It's a win-win for all.

5. By pre-recording, once complete, we had the rest of the term to plan ahead to ensure everything continued to run like clockwork. Then, we were able to make decisions for the next phase without being rushed.

Overall, the positives outweighed the negatives and we were building our business to a level that we would not have achieved if it wasn't for the pandemic, as weird as that might sound. We wouldn't otherwise have had the time to develop such a wonderful support structure as this new component of our wonderful school.

Our ability to stay calm and not make a first decision based on fear was our saving grace. Yes, we did adapt throughout the term and make minor changes, which is just good business practice.

One last decision that was the make or break for our school is worth sharing. On the eve of the Covid-19 closedown, all payment companies had to abide by new legislation requiring that all current customers were to be given written notification if they wanted to continue with any online training. (We run our payment system through a direct debit company.) Without this written declaration, students would not have been able to participate. This legislation was a potential game-changer as the need to have 280 written confirmations from students and parents was almost a death warrant for us, considering the times and everyone's emotional uncertainty. The last thing they would have been worrying about in a pandemic was some need for them to be writing an email for karate classes, and I wouldn't have blamed them.

What did we do?

We stuck to our usual philosophy, which is to consider what might be the best way to move forward for everyone. We noted that some schools developed a new online signup form, but the uncertainty about that was whether everyone would actually go online and do that. I wasn't sure. Instead, we put in the time and drafted individual and personalised letters to each and every student, stating all the changes we had made. Before sending the letters off, over two days we spoke to and comforted every single student/parent, our aim being to provide comfort in our plan, moving forward, and this decision brought a positive light to our karate families during a difficult time. Our conversations and then our letters, delivered a 90% response for continuing, which was exactly what we needed. Day and night we were making calls and having difficult conversations, but it was nothing short of what we owed our customers. The high percentage that continued to train was amazing, and I was proud to have made those decisive and important decisions during that worrying period.

Our online program ran superbly. Of course there were hiccups, just as in every other term of training. We reviewed feedback on our portal and made adjustments where necessary, to ensure we continued to improve our online training. Continuous development: making decisions for the right reasons (not money) and being prepared to think outside the box and commit to hard work. Our difficult but correct decisions left us in a strong position and while solely online training was not perfect—it never will be— we will continue to develop that process and all others, no matter what happens. That's called Business Pivoting, and it never ends ☺

When we run a school, to be successful, we need to always be prepared to strategize and to make decisions for the right reasons, primarily because we love what we do. This advice will always stand us in good stead.

ALL IN ALL...

I leave you with a final question.

What is your passion and why?

I started karate when I was six years old, and at the age of thirteen I decided to compete, with a dream to becoming world champion. This led to the development of my focus on achieving goals.

With a competitive spirit, I would persevere through many obstacles, and over time, perfect my skill (that never ends). Over the next fifteen years I travelled across the world, throughout Europe, and to Morocco, Turkey, and through Asia, and of course to the home of karate: Japan. I learned from the world's best coaches and karate practitioners. The never-ending focus of continuous development led me here today. I learned that I had a passion to help and inspire others to achieve their personal goals in competition, often helping my direct opponents to develop their skills. At the time, I wasn't sure why I enjoyed this element so much but now I get it! Helping others provides a greater satisfaction than helping yourself.

I then opened my first karate school and that led me to the development of the *MEKA KARATE* system, to help others continue their passion and open up their own karate schools. Today, I share my knowledge with the world, with the hope that I am making it a better place. Why? I truly believe the more people in this world that participate in karate the better the world is, and helping others achieve a goal they may never have thought possible gives me a buzz.

I want you to reflect on your own karate journey. Often, we have so much knowledge but lack the self-belief to execute the pathway. If you're reading this book, then I'm sure you have a lot more knowledge than you may think. I suggest reflecting on what you've learned over the years and think about what type of teacher you could become, inspiring students to become strong individuals with strong focus, resilience, commitment, and moral compass. You will mentor them through this period of their lives.

Whether it is running a large karate school or running a school as a hobby, the idea is in the <u>Why?</u> What is your *why* and how are you going to make an impact on this world?

For more information on how to open your own school with our support system, please contact mekakarate@gmail.com

www.ingramcontent.com/pod-product-compliance
Lightning Source LLC
Chambersburg PA
CBHW030847090426
42737CB00009B/1136